How to Make Homemade Bread

Simple and Easy Bread Making Tips and Recipes

Cathy L. Kidd

© 2012 by Cathy L. Kidd

All Rights Reserved. No part of this publication may be reproduced in any form or by any means, including scanning, photocopying, or otherwise without prior written permission of the copyright holder.

First Printing, 2012
Published in the United States of America

Table of Contents

Introduction 1
Homemade Yeast Bread Ingredients and Procedures 3
Conclusion 10

Yeast Bread Recipes 11
    Applesauce and Walnut 11
    Cinnamon Raisin 12
    Cornell Style White 12
    Decorative Lemon 13
    Honey Whole Wheat 14
    Multi-Grain (Wheat, Rye and Oat) 15
    Multi-Grain (Wheat, Rye, Cornmeal, Oatmeal) ...16
    Oatmeal 16
    Oatmeal with Walnuts 17
    Orange Wheat with Nuts 18
    Raisin 19
    Rye (Dark) 20
    Rye (Dark German) 21
    Simple White 22
    Sunflower Seed 22
    Whole Wheat 23
    Whole Wheat with Herbs 24

Quick Bread Recipes 25
    Apple 25
    Apple Pie 25
    Apple with Topping 26
    Apple Rhubarb 27
    Banana 28
    Banana (Lower Sugar) 28
    Banana (Sugarless) 29
    Blueberry Banana 29
    Buttermilk Cheese 30
    Carrot 31
    Cheese 31
    Cheese with Onion Topping 32
    Cranberry Cheese 33
    Lemon 34

  Lemon Cream 35
  Nut 36
  Pimiento Olive 36
  Parmesan Walnut 37
  Pear 38
  Pumpkin 38
  Pumpkin (Lower Sugar) 39
  Rhubarb Pecan 39
  Orange Nut 40
  Walnut 41
  Walnut with Vanilla 41
  Zucchini 42

Specialty Bread Recipes 43
Braids 43
  Chanukah Braid 43
  Chocolate Filled Braid 44
  Egg Braid 46
  Onion Braid 47
  Pumpkin Filled Braid 48
  Tricolor Braid 50
Twists 52
  Molasses Oatmeal 52
  Sour Cream Twist 53
Filled Bread 54
  Cream Cheese 54
  Nut Orange Bread with Honey Filling 56
  Parsley Filled 58
Extras 59
  Hazelnut Flatbread 59
  Mountain Corn Bread 60
  Spoonbread 60

About the Author 61

Introduction

There's nothing quite like making your own homemade bread! Not only is it delicious, nutritious and comforting food, but making it yourself can also save you quite a bit of your grocery money. The price of commercially produced bread has gone up significantly while the ingredients are still low cost. And it doesn't take all that long, so it makes sense to make your own homemade bread.

There are two main types of bread that I've included in this book. The first is traditional yeast bread and the second is quick bread. I have, however, included one flatbread and a couple extras just for fun.

Bread is a very simple, ancient staple food made with flour, water or some other form of liquid, and a leavening agent which lightens the dough and makes it rise. The first forms of bread were no doubt unleavened, flat bread like the Hazelnut Flatbread included in this book. The discovery of the effect of yeast on unleavened dough allowed a lighter, bigger type of loaf to be made. To get that type of loaf, yeast breads require working the dough known as kneading. This kneading allows the fermentation bubbles created by the yeast to be combined with the gluten contained in the flour and thereby kept in the dough. These yeast bubbles are what help give the bread its lightness and form.

Another type of bread was developed most likely in the U.S. at the end of the 18th century. During the Civil War there was a high demand for food produced quickly. The resulting type of bread was called quick bread. It was faster because the leavening agent used was baking soda or powder which produced bread that didn't need kneading and rising time. You'll see in the recipes in this book that all of the quick breads call for baking soda and/or powder and no yeast.

Today, there are two main ways to make homemade bread, by hand and with the help of a bread machine. This book will concentrate on the by hand method. If you have a bread machine or are interested in getting one and using that to make your bread, I suggest you get my book, *Homemade Bread Recipes–A Simple and Easy Bread Machine Cookbook*. The advantage of a bread machine is it does the kneading and rising for you. A benefit in my mind! On the other hand, many people find kneading the bread themselves to be very relaxing and a wonderful stress relieving activity.

So let's get started with the by hand method of homemade bread making and see what we can create!

Homemade Yeast Bread Ingredients and Procedures

The Yeast
The yeast is one of the most critical ingredients so we'll start with that. It's what makes your bread rise and gives it the right consistency – not too soft, not too hard. One thing you may not know is that yeast is a living organism that needs moisture, warmth and food to grow and produce the rising effect for your dough. When you look at homemade bread recipes you'll notice that all three of these elements are included. There's always some form of liquid (water or milk most commonly), and warmth (covering the rising bread with a cloth and putting it in a warm area) and food. Yeast's favorite food is sugar so you'll see that in some form in many recipes. If you don't see sugar, then you'll see warm water and flour which allows the yeast to break down the flour starch into a simple sugar.

The easiest yeast to use is the kind labeled Active Dry Yeast, but any kind will do. Just be sure to check the expiration date so you'll get the best results. Also store it in the refrigerator to keep it as fresh as possible for as long as possible. If you get a flat, dense loaf instead of a light and airy one, look first to the quality of your yeast for the solution.

Note: 1 package of yeast equals 1 Tablespoon.

The Flour
In order for your homemade bread to have the right consistency, you have to choose the right kind of flour. The best is the kind labeled specifically bread flour. It has a higher content of protein or gluten. The presence of gluten is important because it makes your bread more elastic and allows it to rise better to produce a fuller, rounder loaf.

It works by trapping the CO_2 bubbles created by the yeast as it ferments so the dough will rise. Otherwise, the CO_2 would just bubble up to the surface of the dough and be lost and you'd have a flat, very dense loaf.

In a pinch all purpose flour can also be used for most recipes. Some people add an extra tablespoon per cup of flour to compensate. You may need to experiment a bit if you use all purpose instead of bread flour. Note that most of the quick bread recipes just call for flour. You can use all purpose in these cases.

The Liquid
The type of liquid called for in the recipe will determine the kind of bread you get. With water, the crust will be crisper and the bread will have more of a wheat taste to it. Milk will give you a loaf with a richer taste and a finer texture. Also, milk will cause the bread to brown quicker because it adds more sugar and butterfat to the dough. If orange juice is an ingredient, the bread will be sweeter and have less of a grain flavor. If you'd like to experiment a little, you can substitute water for milk and see how it affects the finished bread.

Fats
Shortening, oils or butter will give your homemade bread more flavor and some moisture. On the other hand, the lack of fat in a recipe means it will be a crisper, harder bread like French bread. Don't substitute margarine or whipped butter unless specifically called for because they have a higher amount of water. Too much water will make a loaf that doesn't last very long. Breads made with butter or oil stay fresh longer. That is if it isn't eaten as soon as it comes out of the oven!

Some recipes you find will call for lard as the fat. There's one Whole Wheat Bread recipe in this book that calls for it. The difference between lard and shortening is the primary ingredient it is made from. Lard comes from animal fat and shortening from plant or vegetable oil. You can easily substitute the much easier to find shortening for the lard.

Eggs
If your recipe calls for eggs, your finished loaf will have extra color, flavor and protein. They tend to add richness to the loaf and tenderness to the crust. Some recipes call for an egg wash (made with egg white and water) to add extra color and shine to the finished product.

Salt
Almost all bread recipes will call for salt. You may be tempted to leave it out but salt actually helps with how the yeast develops and acts to keep the bread from rising more than it's supposed to. It also adds flavor. Of course, there are many people on a salt reduced diet. In this case you can try substituting yogurt to help the bread rise normally.

Finishing Touches
In addition to the egg wash mentioned earlier, there are other finishing touches you can do before you bake your bread. If you'd like a crisp and chewy crust, spray a little water on the dough during the baking process. If you'd rather it be softer, brush milk on the dough before baking it. Butter will also make a softer crust. Some of the recipes suggest a topping like nuts or cornmeal that you can put on your bread before baking. These are some ways to experiment with bread crust and make your bread special. Feel free to create your own.

Substituting Ingredients
As previously mentioned you can substitute shortening for lard and yogurt for salt. Another common substitution is applesauce for oil. In most cases you can just substitute equal amounts, but be careful if the recipe calls for more than 1/4 cup of oil. If you substitute that much applesauce it may change the chemistry of the finished loaf. You can also substitute honey for sugar up to one cup. After that again, the finished bread will come out differently.

A couple of the recipes call for buttermilk. You can make your own by combining just under one cup of milk and 1 tablespoon of white vinegar or lemon juice to equal one cup of liquid. Let it stand for 5 minutes and then use the amount called for in the recipe.

Mixing Ingredients
The recipes will tell you exactly how to mix the ingredients to get the best results for each type of bread. In general you will be combining the liquids and yeast in one bowl and the flours in another. Sometimes the yeast will go in with the dry so be sure to read the recipe carefully. You'll then add the liquid to the dry and mix them thoroughly until you have a somewhat sticky dough. If the recipe calls for an electric mixer, be careful! Pieces of the dough can fly everywhere if you mix it too long. Switch to mixing by hand after the ingredients are combined. After you have a fully mixed dough, you'll put on a floured work board to knead.

Kneading the Dough
Start kneading the dough by turning it over several times and folding it in on itself. Use the heels of your hands to push it away from you. Keep doing this until your dough has been smoothed out and feels springy and elastic. If there are specific recommendations for one of the breads, the recipe will tell you how long to work the dough. For the rest of the recipes you can use your best judgment to tell when you've kneaded it enough. You may need to add a little flour to your hands or the board so that the dough does not stick to them.

Letting the Bread Rise
Again each recipe will give you specific directions, but you will do pretty much the same thing for each bread. You'll do a first rise by putting the dough in a lightly greased mixing bowl. Use butter or shortening to grease the bowl. Turn the kneaded dough in the bowl and make sure every part is greased. Greasing keeps the dough from drying out as it rises. Use a clean cloth to cover it. Place it in a warm area and allow the dough to rise. You can place it in a very low oven if you don't have a warm place in your kitchen. Or if you want to watch TV while you wait for it to rise, you can put it on top of the TV. Of course that's assuming you don't have a flat screen!

After this first rise, you'll punch it down and then place it in the pan or on the cookie sheet you'll use to bake it and let it rise again. You'll want to grease these as well.

Baking
Bake your bread for the specified time and at the specified temperature the recipe calls for. When it's done you'll see a golden brown crust. A simple test to see if the bread is done is to tap it with one or two fingers. It should have a hollow sound. Take the bread from the pan and place it on a wire rack to cool. Be sure to enjoy the aroma of your creation. But don't slice it yet! Wait for it to cool completely so you'll get better slices.

Freezing Bread Dough

Some of the recipes in this book make two loaves or very large loaves so you may want to freeze half of the dough for later use. Frozen dough also makes a great gift for a friend who would like homemade bread but isn't a baker like you. There are two procedures you can use to freeze the dough.

The first way is to make the bread according to the recipe directions and let it go through the first rise. Punch it down and form it into loaves. The shape of the loaves doesn't matter too much at this stage because you will re-form it when you're ready to bake it. Wrap the loaves you're going to freeze very tightly with 2 layers of plastic wrap and put them in plastic grocery bags. Tie them securely shut and put them in the freezer.

When you're ready to bake it, let it thaw first in the refrigerator overnight. Remove it from the wrappings and knead it again to be sure it is completely thawed. Re-form the loaf again and put it in a greased pan for the second rise. You may need to let it rise longer than the recipe calls for with fresh dough. After it has risen sufficiently, bake it as usual.

A second way is to bake the loaves you want to freeze according to the recipe directions except take it out about 10 minutes before it would be done. Let the partially cooked loaf cool completely and then wrap it securely and freeze it. In this case you can freeze it in the baking pan if you want. A foil pan works well. When you're ready to use this loaf all you have to do is let it defrost and then bake it the rest of the way.

If you give the dough as a gift, be sure to include the finishing instructions. If you would like to give pretty gift recipe cards, you can download my template and fill them out to give to your friend.
Download them here:
http://www.easyhomemadebreadrecipes.com/RecipeCards.doc

How to Slice Your Homemade Bread
Once the beautiful homemade bread comes out of the oven, many people find they have trouble slicing it without destroying it. Here are some suggestions to try.

First, be sure the loaf is totally cool before starting to slice it. Some people find putting it on its side makes it easier to slice. This works well if the top is crusty.

Use a sharp, serrated knife that is specifically made for slicing bread. It should be long enough so it cuts the length of the loaf in one motion. There are special knives that have wooden or metal guides that you might try. Many people opt for an electric knife using very gentle pressure.

When you start cutting, do it gently and steadily so you get an even slice. You'll know immediately if your knife isn't sharp enough! It takes some practice, but you can always remember that it's what it tastes like that counts – not what it looks like!

Bread Making Equipment
For the recipes in this book you will need a combination of the following items:
- Mixing bowls
- Measuring cups and spoons
- Saucepan
- Electric mixer
- Mixing spoons
- Offset metal spatula (for the Hazelnut Flatbread). This is a metal spatula with a blade that bends up at the handle.
- Thermometer (if you want to be precise about the heated liquid temperatures)
- Baking pans, casserole dishes or cookie sheets

Conclusion

Making homemade bread can be a rewarding experience for you and your family. It's something you can share and do together from the mixing and kneading to of course the best part – the eating! Some of these techniques will take a little practice if you're new to bread making, but that's half the fun, don't you think?

So enjoy and join us at
http://www.easyhomemadebreadrecipes.com
to share your experiences and get more recipes and tips.

All the best,
Cathy

Yeast Bread Recipes

Applesauce and Walnut

–Makes 2 Loaves–

Approx. 6 cups	Flour
1 cup	Whole bran cereal
1 cup	Brown sugar, firmly packed
1/2 teaspoon	Salt
1 teaspoon	Cinnamon
2 packages	Yeast
1/2 cup	Milk
1/3 cup	Water
1/3 cup	Margarine
1 cup	Applesauce, room temperature
2	Eggs, room temperature
1 cup	Walnuts, chopped

Mix together 1 cup flour, the cereal, brown sugar, salt, cinnamon and yeast.
Heat the milk, water and margarine to 120-130 degrees, add to the dry ingredients and beat 2 minutes at medium speed.
Add the applesauce, eggs and 1 cup flour. Beat at high speed 2 minutes.
Stir in walnuts and enough additional flour to make a soft dough.
Cover and let rise in a warm place until doubled, about 1 hour.
Stir batter down and divide equally between two well greased 1 1/4 quart casserole dishes or pans. Cover and let rise until doubled, about 1 hour.
Bake at 350 degrees for 35 minutes or until done.
Remove from casseroles and cool.

Cinnamon Raisin

–Makes 1 Loaf–

2 teaspoons	Yeast
3/4 cup +2 tablespoons	Warm water (110 degrees)
1 tablespoon	Butter, softened
2 cups	Flour
2 tablespoons	Sugar
1 teaspoon	Salt
3/4 teaspoon	Cinnamon powder
1/2 cup	Raisins

Dissolve yeast in warm water.
Stir in all other ingredients.
Knead and let rise until double.
Punch down and form loaf.
Place in greased pan and let rise until double.
Bake at 375 for about 40 minutes.

Cornell Style White

–Makes 2 Loaves–

2 packages	Rapid rise yeast
3 cups	Warm water, 105–115 degrees
1/3 cup	Honey
3-5 cups	All purpose unbleached flour
1/2 cup	Soy flour
3/4 cup	Non fat dry milk powder
3 tablespoons	Wheat germ
2 tablespoons	Oil
2 teaspoons	Salt

Combine the yeast, warm water and honey. Stir to dissolve yeast.
Combine 3 cups flour, the soy flour, milk powder and wheat germ in a large bowl.
Stir in yeast mixture, beat until smooth.
Add oil, salt and enough remaining flour to make a soft dough.

Turn out onto lightly floured surface; knead until smooth and elastic, about 10 minutes.
Please in a greased bowl, turning to grease all sides.
Cover and let rise until double, about 45 minutes.
Punch down, let rise again for 30 minutes.
Punch down, divide dough in half.
Shape into loaves. Place in greased loaf pans.
Cover; let rise until double.
The tops may be brushed with milk and sprinkled with wheat germ prior to baking if desired.
Bake at 350 degrees for 50-55 minutes or until done.
Cool out of pans on wire racks.

Decorative Lemon

This recipe calls for pearl sugar which is a special kind of sugar used in decorative baking. They are white chunks of sugar that will not melt when baking your bread. You can find it online and in specialty grocery stores. If you can't find it, you can use raw sugar which will make the crust sparkle in the light. It's not the same effect, but a nice one nonetheless.

–Makes 1 Loaf–

1 cup	Warm water
1/3 cup	Sugar
1 tablespoon	Active dry yeast
2	Large eggs, lightly beaten
1/4 cup	Vegetable oil
1 teaspoon	Salt
1 tablespoon	Lemon peel, grated
4-4 1/2 cups	Bread flour
1	Egg white mixed with 1 teaspoon water
	Pearl sugar

Combine the warm water and sugar in a large mixing bowl.
Dissolve the yeast in this mixture and let sit until foamy.
Stir in the beaten eggs, oil, salt and lemon peel.
Add 1 1/2 cups of flour and blend well. Beat for 2 minutes.
Add enough remaining flour to make a soft dough.

Turn out dough on a lightly floured surface and knead until smooth and elastic.
Place dough in a greased bowl, turning to coat all sides. Cover and let rise until double.
Punch down dough. Shape as desired to make either a pan or a free loaf.
Place loaf in greased loaf pan or on a greased baking sheet. Cover and let rise until double.
Brush loaf with egg white and sprinkle with pearl sugar.
Bake in preheated 350 degree oven for 30 minutes.
Remove from pan and cool on a wire rack.

Honey Whole Wheat

–Makes 2 Loaves–

1 cup	Milk
1/2 cup	Honey
1 cup	Water
3 tablespoons	Butter flavored shortening
3 1/2 cups	Unbleached flour
2 1/2 cups	Whole wheat flour
1 tablespoon	Salt
2 packages	Yeast
1	Egg
	Butter, melted

Combine in a saucepan the milk, honey, water and shortening. Heat until warm. Set aside to cool.
Mix together in large bowl the flours, salt and yeast.
Add cooled milk mixture to dry ingredients in large bowl.
Add egg. Beat on low speed until moist. Beat on medium for 3 minutes.
Turn out onto floured board and knead until smooth and elastic.
Place in greased bowl turning greased side up and loosely cover with plastic wrap and a damp towel.
Let rise until doubled. Punch down dough, knead again.
Let rise in greased bowl as before.

After the last rising, split the dough in half and place in greased bread pans.
Let rise until double.
Bake about 45 minutes at 375 degrees.
Remove from loaf pans and brush tops with melted butter.

Multi-Grain (Wheat, Rye and Oat)

–Makes 3 Loaves–

4 teaspoons	Salt
1 1/2 packages	Rapid rise yeast
1 cup	Instant nonfat dry milk
3-4 cups	White flour
2 cups	Whole wheat flour
3 cups	Warm water
1/3 cup	Honey
1/3 cup	Oil
1 1/2 cups	Rye flour
1 1/2 cups	Rolled oats

Combine the salt, yeast, dry milk, 2 cups white flour, and 2 cups whole wheat flour in mixer bowl.
Mix well. Add water, honey, and oil.
Mix on low speed until moistened; beat on medium speed 3 minutes.
Add rye flour, rolled oats, and enough white flour to make dough pull away from the sides of bowl.
On a floured surface, knead until smooth and elastic.
Place in a greased bowl, turning once.
Cover and let rise until double, about 30 minutes.
Punch down dough and let rise again, about 25 minutes.
Punch down and shape into 3 loaves.
Place in greased 8" x 4" pans.
Let rise, about 20 minutes.
Bake at 350 for 45 minutes. Turn out of pans and let cool on wire racks.

Multi-Grain (Wheat, Rye, Cornmeal, Oatmeal)

–Makes 3 Loaves–

3 cups	Boiling water
3/4 cup	Cornmeal
1/3 cup	Brown sugar
1/4 cup	Oil
3 tablespoons	Yeast
1 teaspoon	Sugar
1/4 teaspoon	Ginger
3/4 cup	Warm water
1 1/2 tablespoons	Salt
1 1/2 cups	Whole wheat flour
3/4 cup	Rye flour
3/4 cup	Oatmeal
6 cups	Bread flour

Add boiling water to cornmeal, brown sugar, and oil. Let cool.
Add the yeast, sugar, and ginger to warm water. Stir into cooled cornmeal mix.
Add the salt, whole wheat flour, rye, and oatmeal.
Add the bread flour and knead for 8 minutes.
Let rise until double, about 1 hour.
Shape into 3 loaves. Let rise until doubled.
Bake at 350 degrees for 40 minutes.

Oatmeal

–Makes 2 Loaves–

2 tablespoons	Yeast
1/2 cup	Warm water (115 degrees)
2 cups	Rolled oats
2 tablespoons	Butter
2 cups	Boiling water
1/2 cup	Molasses
4 teaspoons	Salt
5 1/2-6 cups	Bread flour
	Egg white and extra oats for topping

Dissolve the yeast in the warm water. Set aside.
In large bowl, place oats and butter. Pour in boiling water. Cool to lukewarm.
Stir in softened yeast, molasses, and salt.
Stir in flour to make a firm dough.
Knead 8 minutes.
Place in greased bowl. Cover and let rise 1 hour.
Divide into 2 loaves. Cover and let rise to double.
Brush with egg white and sprinkle with oats.
Bake at 400 for 35-40 minutes.

Oatmeal with Walnuts

–Makes 2 Loaves–

2 2/3-3 cups	Flour
2 packages	Yeast
2 teaspoons	Salt
1 1/2 cups	Water
1/3 cup	Molasses
4 teaspoons	Shortening
2/3 cup	Rolled oats
1 cup	Walnuts, chopped
1 1/3 cups	Whole wheat flour
1	Egg with 1 tablespoon water
2 tablespoons	Rolled oats

Combine 2 cups flour, the yeast, and salt; mix well.
In saucepan, heat the water, molasses, shortening, and rolled oats until warm.
Add to flour mixture. Mix for 3 minutes.
Stir in walnuts and whole wheat flour.
Add remaining flour to form soft dough.
Knead 5 to 8 minutes.
Cover and let rise 30 minutes.
Divide dough in half. Shape each into round loaf.
Cover and let rise 40 minutes.
Slash top. Brush with egg. Sprinkle with oats if desired.
Bake at 375 for 30 to 35 minutes.

Orange Wheat with Nuts

–Makes 2 Loaves–

3 1/2-4 1/2 cups	All purpose flour
2 packages	Yeast
1 tablespoon	Orange peel, grated
1 1/2 teaspoons	Salt
2 cups	Milk
1/2 cup	Water
1/3 cup	Honey
1/4 cup	Vegetable oil
3 1/2 cups	Whole wheat flour
1 1/2 cups	Walnuts, chopped and toasted

In large bowl, combine 3 cups all purpose flour, the yeast, orange peel and salt.

Heat the milk, water, honey and oil until very warm (120-130 degrees).

Gradually add to dry ingredients; beat 2 minutes at medium speed of electric mixer, scraping bowl occasionally. Beat 2 minutes at high speed.

With a spoon, stir in whole wheat flour, walnuts and enough remaining all purpose flour to make a soft dough.

Knead on lightly floured surface until smooth and elastic, about 6 to 8 minutes.

Place in greased bowl, turning to grease all sides.

Cover and let rise in warm, draft free place until doubled in size, about 30 to 45 minutes.

Punch dough down. Place on a lightly floured surface.

Divide into 6 equal pieces. Form each into a smooth ball.

Grease 2 (8 1/2" X 4 1/2") loaf pans. Place 3 balls in each pan.

Cover; let rise until doubled in size, about 30 to 45 minutes.

Bake at 375 degrees 45 minutes or until done, covering with foil during the last 15 minutes to prevent excess browning.

Remove from pans. Let cool on wire racks.

Raisin

–Makes 3 Loaves–

8- 8 1/2 cups	White flour
2 packages	Yeast
3/4 cup	Sugar
1 tablespoon	Salt
1 1/2 cups	Milk
1/2 cup	Water
3/4 cup	Butter or margarine
4	Eggs
1 cup	Raisins

In a large bowl, combine 3 cups flour, the yeast, sugar, and salt and mix well.
In a saucepan, heat the milk, water, and butter until warm (120-130 degrees). The butter does not need to melt. Add to the flour mixture.
Add the eggs and raisins.
Blend at low speed until moistened then beat 3 minutes at medium speed.
By hand, gradually stir in enough remaining flour to make a firm dough.
Knead on floured surface until smooth and elastic, about 5 minutes.
Place in greased bowl, turning to grease all sides.
Cover and let rise in a warm place until doubled, about 1 1/2 hours.
Punch dough down. Divide into 3 parts. Shape into loaves and put in greased loaf pans.
Cover and let rise in warm place until doubled, about 45 minutes.
Bake at 375 for 25 to 30 minutes until golden brown.
Remove from pans. Cool.

Rye (Dark)

–Makes 2 Loaves–
2 tablespoons	Dry yeast
2 cups	Warm water
1/2 teaspoon	Sugar or honey
1/4 cup	Molasses
1/4 cup	Maple syrup
1/4 cup	Soft sweet butter
1 tablespoon	Salt
2 tablespoons	Cocoa
3-4 cups	Bread flour
3 cups	Rye flour
	Stone ground cornmeal

–GLAZE–
2 tablespoons	Honey
2 tablespoons	Molasses

In large mixing bowl, dissolve the yeast in warm water with sugar or honey. Let sit until bubbly.

Add molasses, maple syrup, soft butter, salt and cocoa. Beat well.

Add 3 cups bread flour and beat 2 minutes with an electric mixer or at least 200 strokes by hand.

Add 3 cups rye flour and mix until the dough leaves the sides of the bowl.

Turn dough out onto a floured surface and knead until smooth and elastic.

Sprinkle with a little white flour if it remains too sticky to handle.

When dough becomes elastic, stop kneading even if dough remains a little clingy to fingers.

Place the dough in a buttered bowl, turn to coat all sides. Cover and let rise until doubled.

Punch dough down, turn out onto board, knead a few times to press out air bubbles, cut in half.

Cover and let rise 10-15 minutes.

Shape the dough into two round or oval loaves and place on a greased baking sheet which has been dusted with cornmeal.
You can cut a design in the tops with a sharp knife.
Cover and let rise until almost double in size.
Brush with glaze.
Bake at 375 degrees for 15 minutes.
Lower the oven temperature to 350 degrees for another 20-25 minutes or until bottoms sound hollow when tapped.
Cool on rack.

Rye (Dark German)

–Makes 2 Loaves–

3 cups	Flour
2 packages	Active dry yeast
1/4 cups	Cocoa powder
1 tablespoon	Caraway seed
2 cups	Water
1/3 cup	Molasses
2 tablespoons	Butter or margarine
1 tablespoon	Sugar
1 tablespoon	Salt
3-3 1/2 cups	Rye flour

In large mixing bowl, combine the flour, yeast, cocoa powder and caraway seed until well blended.
In saucepan, combine water, molasses, butter or margarine, sugar and salt and heat until just warm, stirring occasionally to melt the butter. Add to the dry mixture in mixer bowl.
Beat at low speed with electric mixer for 1/2 minute until mixed. Beat 3 minutes at high speed.
By hand, stir in enough rye flour to make a soft dough.
Turn onto a floured surface, knead until smooth, about 5 minutes.
Cover; let rise, about 20 minutes.
Punch down and divide dough in half. Shape each half into a round loaf and place on greased baking sheets or in two 8" pie plates.

Brush surface of loaves with a little vegetable oil. Slash tops of loaves with sharp knife.
Let rise until double, about 45-60 minutes.
Preheat oven to 400 degrees. Turn to 375 degrees and bake 25-30 minutes or until breads are done.
Remove from pans to wire racks to cool.

Simple White

–Makes 2 Loaves–

2 3/4 cups	Milk
3 tablespoons	Butter
5 3/4-6 1/4 cups	Flour
2 packages	Yeast
2 tablespoons	Sugar
2 teaspoons	Salt

Heat the milk and butter in a medium saucepan (120 degrees).
In a large bowl combine 3 cups flour, the yeast, sugar and salt.
Add the milk mixture. Knead for about 3 minutes.
Add enough of the remaining flour to make a stiff dough.
Knead until the dough is smooth and satiny.
Form into ball and place in a greased bowl, turning it once to grease the entire surface.
Let rise for one hour.
Punch the dough down and divide into 2 sections.
Make into two balls and let the dough rest for 10 minutes.
Shape into two loaves and place in 2 greased 9x5" pans.
Let rise until doubled in size.
Glaze with egg white and seeds if desired.
Bake at 375 for 10 minutes, then at 350 for 30-35 minutes.
Remove from pans and cool on racks.

Sunflower Seed

–Makes 2 Loaves–

2 packages	Yeast
1 1/2 cups	Warm water
1/3 cup	Sugar

3/4 cup	Milk, scaled and cooled
4 tablespoons	Oil
1 teaspoon	Salt
3/4 cup	Sunflower seeds
3-4 cups	Unbleached flour
3 cups	Whole wheat flour

Soften yeast in warm water. Add sugar.
Add milk, oil, salt, sunflower seeds and 1 cup flour.
Stir in wheat flour gradually.
Add enough remaining white flour to make a soft smooth ball.
Knead well.
Cover and let rise until doubled in size.
Punch down dough and shape into 2 loaves.
Cover and let rise until doubled in size.
Bake at 350 degrees until golden brown.

Whole Wheat

–Makes 2 Loaves–

1 tablespoon	Yeast
1/2 cup	Warm water
1/2 cup	Dark brown sugar
1 tablespoon	Salt
1/4 cup	Lard, melted
1 cup	Scalded milk
1 cup	Cool water
3 cups	Flour
3 cups	Whole wheat flour

Soak the yeast in the warm water. Set aside.
In a large mixing bowl, combine the brown sugar, salt and melted lard.
Add the scalded milk and cool water.
Add the yeast mixture.
Mix in the flour, 1 cup of each at a time, stirring and beating until the mixture is heavy enough to put on a bread board to knead.
Knead until you have a smooth elastic dough.

To test for the perfect amount of flour, let dough lay on board with your hands on it.
Count slowly to 30. If the dough does not stick to your hands or board, there is enough flour in it.
Return to bowl. Grease the top and cover with plastic.
Let rise to double, about 2 hours.
Punch down and let rise again for a finer texture.
Shape into 2 loaves.
Put into greased pans. Let rise one hour.
Bake about 45 minutes at 375 degrees.
Your bread is done when it will fall out of the pans.

Whole Wheat with Herbs

–Makes 2 Loaves–

2 tablespoons	Yeast
3 tablespoons	Sugar
1 1/2 cups	Warm water (110-115 degrees)
2 cups	Whole wheat flour
1/3 cup	Dry milk
2 teaspoons	Salt
2 teaspoons	Caraway seeds, crushed
1/2 teaspoon	Nutmeg
1/2 teaspoon	Sage
2 tablespoons	Oil
1	Egg
2 1/2 cups	White flour

Place yeast and sugar in warm water.
Add whole wheat flour, milk, salt, and herbs and beat 30 strokes.
Add oil and egg and beat 75 strokes.
Stir in white flour, turn onto board, and knead.
Let rise in buttered bowl, covered, until doubled.
Punch down and form two loaves.
Let rise until doubled.
Bake about 45 minutes at 375.

Quick Bread Recipes

Apple

–Makes 1 Loaf–

1/2 cup	Shortening
1 cup	Sugar
2	Eggs, beaten
1 1/2 tablespoon	Milk
1 teaspoon	Vanilla
1 teaspoon	Baking soda
2 cups	Flour
1/4 cup	Nuts, chopped
1 cup	Apples, ground

Cream shortening and sugar.
Add beaten eggs. Beat well.
Mix in milk and vanilla.
Sift dry ingredients together and add, mixing thoroughly.
Fold in nuts and apples.
Pour into a greased 9x5x3 inch loaf pan.
Bake in a 350 degree oven for one hour.

Apple Pie

–Makes 1 Loaf–

2 cups	All purpose flour
2 teaspoons	Baking powder
1 teaspoon	Apple pie spice*
1/2 teaspoon	Salt
1/4 teaspoon	Baking soda
2/3 cup	Applesauce, chunky
1/2 cup	Sugar
2	Eggs
1/4 cup	Crisco oil
2 tablespoons	Milk
2 tablespoons	Walnuts, chopped
2 teaspoons	Butter or margarine
1 teaspoon	Brown sugar, packed

*Can substitute 3/4 teaspoon ground cinnamon, dash of ground nutmeg, and dash of ground cloves for apple pie spice.

Mix flour, baking powder, apple pie spice, salt and baking soda in medium mixing bowl.
Combine applesauce, sugar, eggs, Crisco oil, and milk in large mixing bowl. Mix well.
Add dry ingredients.
Beat at medium speed of electric mixer just until combined, scraping bowl occasionally.
Pour into oiled and floured 8" x 4" loaf pan.
Combine walnuts, butter and brown sugar in small mixing bowl.
Mix with fork until crumbly.
Sprinkle down center of loaf.
Bake at 350 degrees for 35 to 45 minutes or until golden brown and a toothpick inserted in the center comes out clean.
Immediately remove from pan. Cool on wire rack.

Apple with Topping

–Makes 2 Loaves–

3	Eggs, slightly beaten
2 cups	Sugar
1 cup	Vegetable oil
1 tablespoon	Vanilla extract
3 cups	All purpose flour
1 teaspoon	Baking soda
1 teaspoon	Cinnamon, ground
4 cups	Apples, pared, cored and chopped
1 cup	Pecans, chopped
–TOPPING–	
2 tablespoons	Sugar
1/2 teaspoon	Cinnamon, ground

Stir together eggs, sugar, oil and vanilla in a medium size bowl until well mixed.
Combine flour, baking soda and cinnamon in another bowl.
Stir dry ingredients into the liquid mixture until mixed.

Stir in apples and pecans.
Divide between two greased and floured loaf pans.
Make topping and sprinkle one-half each on top of loaves.
Bake for 1 hour 10 minutes at 325 degrees, or until a toothpick comes out clean.
Cool in pans 10 minutes.
Remove to wire rack to cool completely.

Apple Rhubarb

–Makes 2 Loaves–

1 1/2 cups	Rhubarb, finely chopped
1 1/2 cups	Apples, chopped
1 1/2 cups	Sugar
1/2 cup	Vegetable oil
1 teaspoon	Vanilla
4	Eggs
3 cups	Flour
1 cup	Nuts, chopped
3 1/2 teaspoons	Baking powder
1 teaspoon	Salt
1 teaspoon	Cinnamon

Mix rhubarb, apples, sugar, oil, vanilla, and eggs in a large bowl.
Stir in remaining ingredients.
Pour into 2 greased loaf pans.
Bake 50 to 60 minutes at 350 degrees or until tested done with a toothpick.
Cool 10 minutes in pans.
Loosen sides of loaves from pan. Remove to wire rack to finish cooling.

Banana

–Makes 1 Loaf–

1/2 cup	Shortening
1 cup	Sugar
2	Eggs
3/4 cup	Banana, very ripe, mashed
1 teaspoon	Vanilla
1 1/4 cups	Flour
3/4 teaspoon	Baking soda
1/2 teaspoon	Salt
1/2 cup	Nuts, chopped (optional)

Cream the shortening and sugar until fluffy.
Add eggs, one at a time, beating well after each addition.
Stir in banana and vanilla.
Mix dry ingredients together and add to banana mixture. Mix well.
Pour into greased loaf or 9x9x2-inch pan.
Bake at 350 degrees for 30 to 35 minutes.

Banana (Lower Sugar)

–Makes 1 Loaf–

2 cups	All purpose flour
1 teaspoon	Baking soda
1 teaspoon	Baking powder
1 1/2 teaspoons	Pumpkin pie spice
2	Bananas, ripe, mashed
6 oz. can	Orange juice, frozen
2	Eggs
1 cup	Raisins
	Nuts (optional)

Mix all dry ingredients together and set aside.
In a separate bowl mix bananas, orange juice and eggs.
Combine with the dry ingredients and mix well. Fold in the nuts and raisins.
Pour in a greased and floured loaf pan.

Bake at 350 - 375 degrees for 30-45 minutes or until a toothpick comes out clean.

Banana (Sugarless)

–Makes 1 Loaf–

1 3/4 cups	Cake flour
2 teaspoons	Baking powder
1/4 teaspoon	Baking soda
1/2 teaspoon	Salt
1/4 cup	Margarine, melted
2	Eggs, beaten
	Liquid sweetener to equal 1/2 cup sugar
1 teaspoon	Vanilla
2	Bananas, medium size, mashed

Sift together flour, baking powder, baking soda and salt.
Add remaining ingredients except bananas.
Stir only until flour mixture is moistened.
Fold in mashed bananas.
Pour into greased 8 x 4 inch loaf pan.
Bake at 350 degrees until top springs back when touched, about an hour.

Blueberry Banana

–Makes 1 Loaf–

2/3 cup	Sugar
1/2 cup	Margarine
2	Eggs
1/4 cup	Light sour cream
2	Large bananas, mashed
1/3 cup	Wheat Flour
1 cup	All purpose flour
2 teaspoons	Baking powder
1 teaspoon	Baking soda
1/4 teaspoon	Salt
1/2 cup	Blueberries

Cream the sugar and margarine.
Add the eggs, light sour cream and bananas and mix thoroughly.
Combine flours, baking powder, baking soda and salt.
Add to creamed mixture stirring until well combined.
Fold in blueberries.
Pour into a greased loaf pan.
Bake at 350 degrees for 1 hour or until toothpick inserted in center of loaf comes out clean.

Buttermilk Cheese

–Makes 1 Loaf–

2 cups	Flour
1/2 teaspoon	Baking soda
1 1/2 teaspoons	Baking powder
2 teaspoons	Dry mustard
1 teaspoon	Salt
1 cup	Cheddar cheese, shredded
1 cup	Buttermilk
1/4 cup	Oil
2	Eggs

In a large bowl, combine dry ingredients and cheese. Set aside.
Beat buttermilk, oil and eggs with rotary beater until well blended.
Add all at once to flour mixture and mix just until moist.
Pour into a greased 9x5x3 inch pan.
Bake at 375 degrees for 45-50 minutes or until a toothpick inserted in center comes out clean.
Cool in pan for 10 minutes.
Invert on rack and cool.

Carrot

–Makes 2 Loaves–

3	Eggs
1 1/2 cups	Vegetable oil
2 cups	Carrots, shredded
1 1/2 cups	Sugar
1 teaspoon	Vanilla
2 tablespoons	Orange peel, grated
3 1/2 cups	Flour
2 teaspoons	Baking soda
1 teaspoon	Baking powder
1 teaspoon	Salt
1 teaspoon	Cinnamon
1 teaspoon	Cloves
2/3 cup	Nuts, chopped

Beat eggs, oil, carrots, sugar, vanilla and orange peel with mixer on low speed for one minute, scraping bowl occasionally.
Add flour, baking soda, baking powder, salt, cinnamon and cloves.
Beat on low speed about 15 seconds until moistened, scraping bowl occasionally.
Beat on medium speed for 45 seconds. Stir in nuts.
Spread in 2 greased and floured loaf pans.
Bake at 350 degrees until toothpick inserted in center comes out clean, about 55 to 60 minutes.
Cool ten minutes, remove from pans.
Cool completely before slicing.

Cheese

–Makes 1 Loaf–

2 cups	Flour
1/4 cup	Sugar
1/2 teaspoon	Baking soda
1 1/2 teaspoons	Baking powder
2 teaspoons	Dry mustard

2 tablespoons	Parmesan cheese, grated
1/2 teaspoon	Chili powder
1/2 teaspoon	Garlic salt
1/2 teaspoon	Onion salt
2	Eggs
1 cup	Buttermilk
1/2 cup	Vegetable oil
2 cups	Cheese, Kraft Mexican, grated

Combine the dry ingredients in a small bowl and set aside.
In a large mixing bowl, beat eggs, buttermilk, and oil.
Add cheese and mix well.
Add dry ingredients all at once.
By hand, blend just until all is moist.
Pour into a prepared 8" x 4" x 2" loaf pan.
Bake at 350 degrees for 45 to 50 minutes or until a toothpick comes out clean.
Cool in pan for 10 minutes, then remove and cool completely before slicing.

Cheese with Onion Topping

–Makes 1 Loaf–

2 cups	Flour
1/4 cup	Sugar
1 1/2 teaspoons	Baking powder
1/2 teaspoon	Baking soda
1/2 teaspoon	Salt
1	Egg, separated and beaten
1 cup	Buttermilk
1 cup	Cheddar cheese, grated
1/4 cup	Onion, chopped
1 tablespoon	Butter

Mix together dry ingredients.
Add beaten egg yolk and milk.
Quickly fold in stiffly beaten egg white and cheese.
Pour into greased loaf pan or round 9" casserole.
Sauté onion in butter.

Spread top with onion mixture.
Bake at 400 degrees for 45 minutes or until top is golden.

Cranberry Cheese

–Makes 1 Loaf–

2 cups	Flour
1 cup	Sugar
1 1/2 teaspoons	Baking powder
1/2 teaspoon	Baking soda
1/2 teaspoon	Salt
2 teaspoons	Orange peel, grated
2 tablespoons	Shortening
1/2 cup	Water
1/4 cup	Orange juice
1 1/2 cups	Cheddar cheese, shredded
1	Egg, beaten
1 cup	Cranberries, halved
1/3 cup	Walnuts, chopped

Measure flour, sugar, baking powder, baking soda, salt and orange peel into a bowl.
Cut in shortening.
Add water and juice. Mix with cheese and egg.
Combine with flour mixture.
Stir in cranberries and nuts.
Pour into greased 9x5x3 loaf pan.
Bake at 350 degrees for 60-70 minutes or until done.
Cool, remove from pan
Let loaf stand at least 8 hours before cutting.

Lemon

–Makes 1 Loaf–

3/4 cup	Butter, softened
1 1/4 cups	Sugar
3	Eggs
2 1/4 cups	Flour
1/4 teaspoon	Salt
1/4 teaspoon	Baking soda
3/4 cup	Buttermilk
1 1/2 teaspoons	Lemon rind, grated
3/4 cup	Nuts, chopped

–LEMON GLAZE–

1/2 cup	Lemon juice
3/4 cup	Confectioner's sugar

Beat together butter and sugar in large bowl until light and fluffy.
Add eggs; mix well.
Sift together flour, salt, and baking soda.
Add to butter mixture alternating with buttermilk, beating well after each addition.
Stir in lemon rind and nuts.
Pour into greased and floured 9" loaf pan.
Bake at 300 degrees for 1 1/2 hours.
Cool bread in pan for 15 minutes. Turn bread out onto wire rack.

Prepare Lemon Glaze:
Stir lemon juice into confectioner's sugar in bowl until sugar dissolves.
Pierce top of loaf with wooden pick at 1/2" intervals.
Spoon glaze over top of bread while still warm.

Lemon Cream

–Makes 1 Loaf–

1/2 cup	Butter
1 1/4 cups	Sugar
8 oz	Cream cheese
2	Large eggs
2 1/4 cups	All purpose flour
3 teaspoons	Baking powder
1 teaspoon	Salt
5 1/2 oz	Evaporated milk
1/4 cup	Water
1/2 cup	Pecans, chopped
2 tablespoons	Lemon rind, grated

–LEMON GLAZE–

1/3 cup	Sugar
1/4 cup	Lemon juice

Cream butter, sugar, and cream cheese until light and fluffy.
Add eggs, one at a time, beating thoroughly after each one.
Combine the dry ingredients. Combine the milk and water.
Add them to the butter mixture alternating dry and wet, blending well.
Fold in nuts and lemon rind.
Pour into a greased and floured 9x5x3 inch loaf pan.
Bake at 350 degrees about 1 hour or until golden brown.

Prepare Lemon Glaze:
Stir sugar with lemon juice until dissolved.
Drip over hot loaf. Let stand in pan for 30 minutes.
Turn out on a cake rack.

Nut

–Makes 1 Loaf–

2 1/2 cups	Flour
1/2 cup	Sugar
1/2 cup	Brown sugar
3 1/2 teaspoons	Baking powder
1 teaspoon	Salt
3 tablespoons	Vegetable oil
1 1/4 cups	Milk
1	Egg
1/2 cup	Pecans, chopped
1/2 cup	Almonds, chopped
1/2 cup	Brazil nuts, chopped

Mix dry ingredients together.
Add remaining ingredients.
Bake in greased pan at 350 degrees for 55 to 65 minutes.

Pimiento Olive

Pictured on book cover
–Makes 1 Loaf–

2 1/2 cups	Flour
1/4 cup	Sugar
3 teaspoons	Baking powder
3/4 teaspoon	Salt
1 cup	Milk
1	Large egg
1/4 cup	Butter, melted
1 cup	Pimiento stuffed green olives, sliced

Combine flour, sugar, baking powder, and salt. Blend thoroughly.
In a separate bowl, whisk together milk, egg, and melted butter.
Pour egg mixture into the dry ingredients. Beat until well moistened.
Stir in the olives.
Pour into a greased 8" x 2" loaf pan

Bake for 50 minutes to 1 hour at 350 degrees, covering it with foil during last 10 minutes if necessary.
When a toothpick comes out clean, remove and let stand 10 minutes before removing from pan.

Parmesan Walnut

–Makes 1 Loaf–

3 cups	All purpose flour
2/3 cup	Sugar
1/2 cup	Parmesan cheese, grated
4 teaspoons	Baking powder
1/2 teaspoon	Salt
1	Egg, beaten
1 3/4 cups	Milk
1/3 cup	Walnut oil
1 cup	Walnuts, chopped

In a large mixing bowl, combine the flour, sugar, cheese, baking powder, and salt.
In a small bowl, stir together the egg, milk, and oil
Add to flour mixture, stirring just until combined.
Stir in 3/4 cup of the nuts.
Turn into a greased 9" x 5" x 3" loaf pan.
Sprinkle with remaining nuts over top.
Bake at 350 degrees for 1 hour or until a toothpick inserted in center comes out clean.
Cool in pan for 10 minutes.
Remove loaf from the pan and cool completely on a wire rack.
Wrap and store overnight before slicing.

Pear

Low sugar recipe
–Makes 2 Loaves–

3 cups	Flour
1 teaspoon	Baking soda
1/4 teaspoon	Baking powder
1 teaspoon	Salt (optional)
1 tablespoon	Cinnamon
1 cup	Pecans, chopped
3/4 cup	Vegetable oil
3	Eggs, slightly beaten
18 packages	Artificial sweetener
2 cups	Pears peeled, grated
2 teaspoons	Vanilla

Combine first six ingredients in large bowl.
Make a well in center and add oil, eggs, sweetener, pears and vanilla.
Stir just until moist.
Put into 2 greased loaf pans.
Bake at 325 degrees for 1 hour and 15 minutes or until tests done.

Pumpkin

–Makes 1 Loaf–

3 1/2 cups	Flour
3 cups	Sugar
1 1/2 teaspoons	Salt
2 cans	Pumpkin
4	Eggs
2 teaspoons	Baking powder
1 teaspoon	Cinnamon
1 teaspoon	Baking soda
1 teaspoon	Cloves, ground
2/3 cup	Water
1 cup	Nuts, chopped

Mix all ingredients until well blended.
Bake in a loaf pan at 350 degrees for 1 to 1 1/2 hours until done.

Pumpkin (Lower Sugar)

–Makes 1 Loaf–

1/2 cup	Pumpkin
1 oz.	Bread
2/3 cup	Dry skim milk powder
2	Eggs
3 packs	Artificial sweetener
1/2 teaspoon	Baking soda
1/4 teaspoon	Cream of tartar
1/2 teaspoon	Cinnamon
1/4 teaspoon	Nutmeg
1/4 teaspoon	Ginger
1/8 teaspoon	Cloves
1/2 teaspoon	Orange rind, grated

Mix all ingredients in bowl with electric mixer until smooth.
Pour into Pam sprayed loaf pan.
Bake at 350 degrees for 30 to 45 minutes.

Rhubarb Pecan

–Makes 2 Loaves–

1 1/2 cups	Brown sugar
2/3 cup	Vegetable oil
1	Egg
1 cup	Buttermilk
1 teaspoon	Baking soda
2 1/2 cups	Flour
1 1/2 cups	Fresh rhubarb, diced
1/2 cup	Pecans, chopped

–TOPPING–

1/2 cup	Sugar
1 tablespoon	Butter

Combine the brown sugar, oil, egg, buttermilk, baking soda, flour, rhubarb and pecans.
Pour into 2 greased and lightly floured loaf pans.
Mix topping ingredients together and sprinkle over batter.
Bake at 350 degrees for 1 hour.

Orange Nut

–Makes 1 Loaf–

1	Orange rind, peeled
1 cup	Raisins
1 cup	Pecans
1 cup	Orange juice, heated
1 teaspoon	Baking soda
1 cup	Sugar
1 teaspoon	Vanilla
1	Egg, beaten
2 cups	Flour
1 teaspoon	Baking powder
1/4 teaspoon	Salt

Grind the orange rind, raisins, and pecans using the finest blade on a food processor and transfer to a bowl.
Pour in the heated orange juice.
Mix in the remaining ingredients.
Mix well and pour into a greased loaf pan.
Bake for 50 minutes at 350 degrees.

Walnut

–Makes 1 Loaf–

3 cups	Flour
1 cup	Sugar
4 teaspoons	Baking powder
1 1/2 teaspoons	Salt
1	Egg
1 1/2 cups	Milk
2 tablespoons	Vegetable oil
3/4 cup	Walnuts, chopped

Mix dry ingredients together.
Combine egg, milk, and oil.
Add to dry ingredients, beating well.
Stir in nuts. Pour into greased loaf pan.
Bake at 350 degrees for 1 to 1 1/2 hours.

Walnut with Vanilla

–Makes 1 Loaf–

3 cups	All purpose flour
1 cup	Sugar
4 teaspoons	Baking powder
2 teaspoons	Salt
1	Egg, lightly beaten
1/4 cup	Shortening, melted
1 1/2 cups	Milk
1 teaspoon	Vanilla
1 1/2 cups	Walnuts, chopped

Combine flour, sugar, baking powder, and salt.
Add egg, shortening, milk and vanilla to dry mixture.
Stir just until all the flour is moistened.
Stir in walnuts.
Pour into greased 9" x 5" x 3" loaf pan.
Bake at 350 degrees for 1 hour and 10 minutes to 1 hour and 20 minutes.

Zucchini

–Makes 2 Loaves–

3	Eggs
2 cups	Sugar
1 cup	Vegetable oil
1 teaspoon	Vanilla
2 cups	Zucchini, peeled and grated
3 cups	Flour
1 teaspoon	Salt
3 teaspoons	Cinnamon
1 teaspoon	Baking soda
1/4 teaspoon	Baking powder
1 cup	Pecans

Beat the eggs, sugar, and vegetable oil together.
Add the vanilla and stir in zucchini.
Combine the flour, salt, cinnamon, baking soda, and baking powder together.
Stir into the egg/sugar mixture.
Mix in the pecans.
Pour into two well greased loaf pans.
Bake at 325 degrees for 60 to 70 minutes.

Specialty Bread Recipes

Braids

Chanukah Braid

–Makes 2 Loaves–

3 tablespoons	Sugar
4 packages	Rapid rise yeast
2 1/2 cups	Warm water
8-9 cups	Flour
1 teaspoon	Salt
3	Eggs, lightly beaten
4 tablespoons	Corn or vegetable oil

–GLAZE–

1	Egg yolk
2 tablespoons	Water
1/2 cup	Sesame or poppy seeds

Mix the sugar, yeast and 1/2 cup water together in small bowl and set aside.
In a large mixer bowl, add 5 cups flour and the salt.
Mix in the yeast mixture, remaining water, eggs and oil.
Add remaining flour to make a smooth dough.
Knead on a floured surface and let rise until double in size.
Punch it down and knead it again.
Divide the dough in half and then divide each half into 3 pieces.
Form the dough into a braid and let rise until doubled.
Combine the egg yolk and water and brush the loaves with the mixture.
Cover with seeds.
Bake at 375 degrees for 45 minutes or until golden brown.

Chocolate Filled Braid

–Makes 1 Loaf–

2 1/4 cups	Bread flour
2 tablespoons	Sugar
1/2 teaspoon	Salt
1 package	Yeast
1/2 cup	Milk
1/4 cup	Water
1/2 cup	Butter

–CHOCOLATE FILLING–

3/4 cup	Mini chocolate chips
2 tablespoons	Sugar
1/3 cup	Evaporated milk
1/2 cup	Walnuts or pecans, finely chopped
1 teaspoon	Vanilla
1/4 teaspoon	Cinnamon

–CONFECTIONERS SUGAR GLAZE–

1 cup	Confectioners sugar
1 tablespoon	Butter or margarine
1/2 teaspoon	Vanilla
2 tablespoons	Milk

Prepare Chocolate Filling and set aside:
Combine chocolate chips, sugar and evaporated milk in small saucepan.
Cook over low heat stirring constantly until chips are melted and mixture is smooth.
Stir in nuts, vanilla and cinnamon. Cool.

For the dough:
Combine 1 cup flour, the sugar, salt and yeast in large bowl and set aside.
Combine the milk, water and butter in saucepan and cook over low heat until very warm (120-130 degrees) the butter does not need to melt.
Add to dry ingredients, beat 2 minutes on medium speed.
Add enough flour to make a stiff dough.
Cover and allow to rest for 20 minutes.

Turn dough onto a well floured board and roll into an 18x10 rectangle.
Spread with chocolate filling lengthwise down the center third of the dough.
Cut 1" wide strips diagonally along both sides of filling to within 3/4" of filling.
Alternately fold opposite strips of dough at an angle across filling.
Transfer to a greased cookie sheet.
Shape into ring stretching slightly and pinch ends together.
Cover with wax paper brushed with vegetable oil and top with plastic wrap.
Chill 1 1/2-2 hours or overnight.
Let dough stand uncovered at room temperature for 10 minutes.
Bake at 375 degrees for 30-35 minutes or until lightly browned.
Remove from baking sheet and cool on wire rack.
Brush with melted butter or drizzle with Confectioners Sugar Glaze.

Confectioners Sugar Glaze:
Beat confectioners sugar, butter, vanilla and milk in small bowl, until glaze is smooth and of desired consistency.

Egg Braid

–Makes 2 Loaves–

2 packages	Yeast
2 cups	Warm water
1/4 cup	Sugar
4 teaspoons	Salt
1/4 cup	Shortening, melted
3	Eggs, slightly beaten (reserve 2 tablespoons for glaze)
3-5 cups	Flour

In a large bowl soften the yeast in the warm water.
Add sugar, salt and shortening.
Blend in eggs (except reserved 2 tablespoons) and 3 cups flour.
Beat well.
Gradually add 4 1/2 to 5 cups flour to form a stiff dough.
Knead on floured surface until smooth and satiny, 7 to 10 minutes.
Place in greased bowl and cover.
Let rise until doubled in size, about 1 1/2 hours.
Divide dough in half and each half in three parts.
Roll each part into a strip about 14" long.
Braid the three strips together, sealing ends.
Place braid in well greased pan. Cover.
Repeat.
Let rise until light and doubled in size, about 45 to 60 minutes.
Brush reserved egg on top of loaves. Put seeds on if desired.
Bake at 375 degrees for 40 to 45 minutes until golden.

Onion Braid

–Makes 2 Loaves–

4 cups	Flour
1/4 cup	Sugar
1 teaspoon	Salt
1 1/2 teaspoons	Yeast
3/4 cup	Water
1/2 cup	Milk
1/4 cup	Butter
1	Egg
2 tablespoons	Cornmeal

–FILLING–

1/2 cup	Butter, softened
1 cup minced onion	Onion, finely chopped or 1/4 cup instant
1 tablespoon	Parmesan cheese, grated
1 tablespoon	Sesame or poppy seed
1 teaspoon	Dill
1 teaspoon	Garlic salt
1 teaspoon	Paprika
1 sprig	Parsley

In a large bowl blend 2 cups flour, the sugar, salt, and yeast.
In a saucepan, heat the water, milk and butter until warm (120-130 degrees).
Add warmed liquid and egg to flour mixture.
Beat for 4 minutes at medium speed.
Stir in remaining flour and knead 10 minutes.
Cover and let rise 45 to 60 minutes.
Grease 2 cookie sheets and sprinkle with cornmeal.
Mix filling ingredients in a large bowl and set aside.
Roll dough to an 18" x 12" rectangle.
Spread with filling.
Cut into six strips.
Start with the longer side and roll and seal edges to create long rolls.
Braid 3 rolls together and seal. Repeat with other three.
Cover braids and let rise 45 to 60 minutes.

Bake at 350 degrees 30 to 35 minutes or until brown.
After baking 20 minutes, brush with egg wash and sprinkle with seed, if desired.

Pumpkin Filled Braid

–Makes 1 Loaf–
1 tablespoon	Yeast
1/2 cup	Warm water
4 1/4 cups	Flour
1/4 cup	Sugar
1 teaspoon	Salt
1 teaspoon	Orange rind, grated
1 cup	Butter, softened
6	Eggs

–FILLING–
1 1/2 cups	Pumpkin, canned, not pie filling
4 oz	Almond paste
1/2 cup	Butter
3/4 cup	Brown sugar, firmly packed
1/8 teaspoon	Nutmeg
1/8 teaspoon	Cloves
1/8 teaspoon	Ginger
1/2 cup	Almonds, toasted, chopped
1/2 teaspoon	Cinnamon
	Cornstarch

–ICING–
2 cups	Powdered sugar
3 tablespoons	Milk
1/2 teaspoon	Almond extract or orange flavoring, if desired
1/4 cup	Almonds, toasted, sliced

Dissolve yeast in warm water in a large mixing bowl.
Add three cups flour, sugar, salt, orange rind, butter and eggs. Beat at low speed until blended. Beat four minutes at medium speed.
Add remaining flour and continue beating at low speed until blended.

Cover dough and let rise in warm place until doubled.
Punch down, cover and refrigerate at least eight hours.

Prepare filling: Combine pumpkin, almond paste, butter, brown sugar, spices and 1/4 cup of the toasted almonds. Stir until blended. Add cornstarch as needed to thicken mixture to about the consistency of a pudding. Set aside.

Punch dough down and divide in thirds.
Roll each section on a floured board to a rectangle approximately 10 inches by 16 inches.
Spread the dough with a thin layer of the filling.
Sprinkle with remaining 1/4 cup of almonds.
Roll each rectangle up as a jelly roll lengthwise and seal edges together well.
Braid the three sections and tuck ends under.
Hint for braiding: Lay the three rolls side by side and braid from the middle to each end.

Place on a baking sheet, cover and let rise until doubled.
Bake at 350 degrees for 15 minutes, until golden brown.
Remove from oven and allow to cool.

Prepare icing: Combine powdered sugar, milk and almond extract or orange flavoring until well mixed. Drizzle over warm braid. Sprinkle with toasted, sliced almonds and drizzle additional icing over almonds to hold them in place.

Tricolor Braid

–Makes 2 Loaves–

2 packages	Active dry yeast
2 1/2 cups	Warm water (110 degrees)
2 tablespoons	Honey
1 tablespoon	Salt
4 tablespoons	Butter, softened
5 cups	All purpose flour
4 tablespoons	Dark molasses
2 tablespoons	Wheat germ
1 1/3 cups	Whole wheat flour
2 tablespoons	Cocoa
1 1/2 teaspoons	Caraway seeds
1 1/3 cups	Rye flour
1	Egg yolk beaten with 1 tablespoon water

In a large bowl, dissolve yeast in water.
Stir in honey, salt, butter and 2 1/3 cups of all purpose flour, beat on high speed for 4 minutes.
Divide batter into thirds, 1 1/2 cup each and place into separate bowls.

Whole Wheat Braid: To 1/3 of dough, add 2 tablespoons molasses, wheat germ and whole wheat flour. Turn out onto a floured board and knead until smooth, about 5 minutes. Add flour as needed to prevent sticking. Place dough in a greased bowl, turn to grease all sides.

Pumpernickel Braid: To 1/3 of dough, stir in remaining 2 tablespoons molasses, cocoa, caraway seeds and rye flour. Turn dough out onto the floured board and knead until smooth, about 5 minutes. Add all purpose flour as needed to prevent sticking. Place dough in a greased bowl, turn to grease all sides.

White Braid: To remaining 1/3 of dough, stir in 1 1/3 cups all purpose flour. Turn dough onto floured board and knead until smooth, about 5 minutes. Add all purpose flour as needed to prevent sticking. Place dough in a greased bowl, turn to grease all sides.

Cover all bowls and let rise in warm place until doubled.
Punch dough down and divide each into half.
Roll each portion into a smooth 15 inch rope.
For each loaf place a white, wheat and pumpernickel rope on a greased 14x17 baking sheet.
Braid loosely, pinch ends to seal, tucking them underneath.
Cover lightly and let rise in a warm place until doubled.

Brush both loaves with egg yolk mixture.
Bake at 350 degrees 35 minutes or until well browned.
To bake both loaves in one oven, place racks in middle of oven, stagger pans and switch pan positions halfway through baking.
Cool on racks.

Twists

Molasses Oatmeal

–Makes 2 Loaves–

6 cups	Flour
2 cups	Oats
1 teaspoon	Salt
2 packages	Yeast
1 cup	Water
1/2 cup	Milk
1/2 cup	Molasses
1/2 cup	Butter or margarine
2	Eggs

In a mixing bowl combine 4 1/2 cups flour, the oats, salt, and yeast.
Combine the water, milk, molasses, and butter or margarine in a saucepan and heat (120-130 degrees). Let the milk mixture cool.
With an electric mixer on medium, gradually add the liquids to flour mixture.
Beat for 2 minutes.
Add the eggs and 3/4 cup of flour and beat for another 2 minutes.
Stir in enough additional flour to make a soft dough.
Turn out the dough and knead for 8-10 minutes.
Place the dough into a greased bowl, turning the dough to grease the top. Cover and let rise for 1 hour.
Punch down the dough and turn out onto lightly floured surface.
Divide the dough into 4 equal parts.
Take 2 sections and roll into 12" ropes, twist them together, turn the ends under, and place in 8.5" x 4.5" x 2.5" loaf pan. Repeat for remaining dough.
Cover the loaf pans and let rise 1 hour.
Bake at 400 degrees for approximately 30 minutes.
A toothpick should come out clean when the bread is done.
Put the loaves out on a cooling rack.

Sour Cream Twist

–Makes 2 Loaves–

1 package	Yeast
1/4 cup	Warm water (120-130 degrees)
4 cups	Flour
1 cup	Butter, melted
1 cup	Sour cream
2	Eggs, slightly beaten
1 teaspoon	Salt
1 teaspoon	Vanilla
1 cup	Sugar
1 teaspoon	Cinnamon

Sprinkle the yeast onto the warm water and stir until well dissolved.
Mix in large bowl, butter, sour cream, eggs, salt, vanilla and yeast mixture.
Add flour slowly and mix until smooth.
Brush with melted butter and cover with a damp cloth.
Refrigerate for at least 2 hours. (May be refrigerated for up to two days).
Combine sugar and cinnamon and sprinkle 1/2 on a board.
Divide the dough into two equal parts.
Knead one part gently in the sugar and cinnamon and roll out a 10 by 15 inch rectangle turning until both sides are coated with sugar mixture.
Fold the long side over three times.
Cut into 15, one inch strips.
Twist each strip and place on well greased baking sheet.
Repeat with the remaining half of the dough and sugar mixture.
Bake 375 degrees for 15 minutes.

Filled Bread

Cream Cheese

–Makes 4 Loaves–

1 cup	Sour cream
1/2 cup	Sugar
1 teaspoon	Salt
1/2 cup	Margarine, melted
2 packages	Yeast
1/2 cup	Warm water
2	Eggs, beaten
4 cups	Flour

–FILLING–

2 packages (8-oz)	Cream cheese
3/4 cup	Sugar
1	Egg, beaten
1/8 teaspoon	Salt
2 teaspoon	Vanilla

–GLAZE FROSTING–

2 cups	Powdered sugar
4 tablespoons	Milk
2 teaspoons	Vanilla

For the dough:
Heat sour cream over low heat.
Stir in sugar, salt and margarine. Cool to lukewarm.
Sprinkle yeast over warm water in large bowl stirring until yeast dissolves.
Add sour cream mixture, eggs and flour. Mix well.
Cover and refrigerate overnight.
Next day divide dough into 4 equal parts.

For the filling:
Combine cream cheese and sugar in small bowl.
Add beaten egg, salt and vanilla and mix well.

Roll each part of the dough into a 12 x 8 inch rectangle.
Spread 1/4 of cream cheese filling on each rectangle.

Roll up jellyroll fashion beginning at long side.
Pinch edges together and fold ends under slightly.
Place seam side down on a greased baking sheet.
Slit each roll at 2" intervals about 2/3 way through dough.
Cover and let rise 1 hour in warm place.
Bake at 375 degrees 12-15 minutes.
Cool slightly and then spread with glaze.

For the Glaze:
Mix all ingredients together.

Nut Orange Bread with Honey Filling

–Makes 1 Loaf–

4 1/2 cups	Flour
2 packages	Rapid rise yeast
2 teaspoons	Salt
1/4 cup	Sugar
1 cup	Milk
1/4 cup	Water
1/2 cup	Butter
2	Eggs, beaten
	Melted butter

–HONEY FILLING–

1/2 cup	Honey
1/4 cup	Sugar
	Peel of 1 orange, grated
1 tablespoon	Orange juice
1 teaspoon	Cinnamon
1/3 cup	Nuts, finely chopped
1 tablespoon	Melted butter

Mix 3 1/2 cups flour, the yeast, salt and sugar in large bowl.
Heat the milk, water and butter until very warm (125-130 degrees).
Stir warm liquid into dry mixture.
Mix in eggs.
Add up to 1 cup flour to make a soft dough.
Knead until smooth and elastic.
Cover dough, let rise 10 minutes.
Make honey filling by combining all ingredients well.

Divide dough in half, keeping the dough that you are not using covered.
Roll out half of the dough into a 16x12" rectangle.
Brush with melted butter and spread with half of the honey filling.
Roll jelly roll fashion, sealing the edges.
Cut into 1" slices.

Place layer in greased 10" tube pan, placing cut side down so they barely touch.

Arrange remaining slices in layers, covering up the spaces, with no slice directly on top of another.

Prepare remaining half of dough in same manner, placing slices on top of layers as before.

Cover and let rise in warm place until doubled, about 1 hour.

Bake in moderate 350 degree oven for 45-60 minutes or until sides and top are well browned.

If the bread browns too soon, cover it with foil for the last half of baking.

Loosen bread from pan, turn out on rack to cool.

Brush top with honey. Serve with butter.

Parsley Filled

–Makes 2 Loaves–

1 package	Active dry yeast
1 tablespoon	Sugar
1 cup	Warm water (105-115 degrees)
2 tablespoons	Vegetable oil
1 teaspoon	Salt
1/2 cup	Wheat germ
1/4 cup	Dry milk
2 1/4-3 cups	Flour

–FILLING–

1 cup	Parsley, chopped
1/4 cup	Green onions, chopped
2	Garlic cloves, minced
1/2 teaspoon	Black pepper
2 tablespoons	Soft butter or margarine
2 tablespoons	Dijon style mustard

Dissolve the yeast and sugar in the warm water.
When the yeast begins to bubble, add the oil, salt, wheat germ, dry milk and flour.
Mix well and knead until a soft dough is formed.
Place in a greased bowl, cover and let rise until light, up to 1 hour.
While the dough is rising, mix together the filling ingredients until well blended.
Cut the dough in half. Roll each half into a rectangle 1/4" thick.
Spread with filling. Roll up tightly tapering the ends.
Make 3-4 gashes in the top of each loaf.
Let rise about 30 minutes or until the loaves are puffy.
Bake at 375 degrees for 30 minutes or until golden.
Cool on wire rack.

Extras

Hazelnut Flatbread

Notice there is no yeast or baking soda/powder so it will be flat

–Makes 8 Servings–
1 cup + 2 tablespoons	All purpose flour
1 1/2 cups	Cocoa powder, unsweetened
1/2 cup	Sugar
3/4 cup	Hazelnuts, toasted, finely chopped
2 cups	Coffee, cooled to room temperature
1/4 cup	Frangelico

Put the flour, cocoa, and sugar in a large bowl and stir together.
Stir in the nuts.
Gradually stir in the coffee and Frangelico until smooth.

Lightly grease a 12-inch by 18-inch cookie sheet to anchor the paper and line it with parchment paper. Lightly grease the paper.
With an offset metal spatula, spread half of the batter onto the cookie sheet in an even 1/16-inch thick layer.
Repeat with the remaining batter on another cookie sheet.
Bake at 350 degrees for 15 minutes, or until crisp.
Set on a rack to cool.
To serve, break the sheets into pieces.

Mountain Corn Bread

–Makes 1 Loaf–

1 1/2 cups	Cornmeal
1/2 cup	Flour
2 teaspoons	Baking powder
1 teaspoon	Baking soda
1 teaspoon	Salt
1	Egg, beaten
2 cups	Buttermilk
1/4 cup	Butter, melted
2 tablespoons	Sugar

Combine dry ingredients and mix well.
Add buttermilk, egg and butter.
Stir until moistened but don't beat.
Pour into greased 8" square pan.
Bake at 425 degrees for 20 to 25 minutes or until golden brown.

Spoonbread

–Makes 1 Loaf–

2 cups	Cornmeal
2 1/2 cups	Boiling water
2	Egg yolks
1 teaspoon	Baking powder
1 teaspoon	Salt
3 tablespoons	Butter, melted
1 1/2 cups	Buttermilk
2	Egg whites, stiffly beaten

Gradually stir the cornmeal into the boiling water.
After the cornmeal mixture has cooled add the egg yolks, baking powder, salt, melted butter, and the buttermilk.
Fold in the beaten egg whites.
Pour into a greased baking pan and bake for 45 minutes at 425 degrees.

About the Author

Cathy L. Kidd is a craftsperson at heart. For as long as she can remember she has been creating things with her hands. She has done crochet (taught to her by her Aunt Carol), stained glass (learned by taking a class), candlemaking (learned from an ebook and experimenting) and homemade bread making first by hand and then with the use of a bread machine (learned initially with the help of Betty Crocker!) She especially likes taking "raw materials" like colored string or flour and water and creating a beautiful gift from them.

This book and her first, *Homemade Bread Recipes – A Simple and Easy Bread Machine Cookbook* have come out of her enjoyment of homemade bread making and the recipes she's found. She especially enjoys taking bread to dinner gatherings with friends and suspects she's invited **because** of the bread she makes!

Her other books inclue:
- Homemade Soup Recipes: Simple and Easy Slow Cooker Recipes
- How to Make Homemade Ice Cream: Simple and Easy Ice Cream Maker Recipes
- How to Make Smoothies: Simple, Easy and Healthy Blender Recipes
- Dehydrating Food: Simple and Easy Dehydrator Recipes

For more recipes, tips and ideas, visit:
www.easyhomemadebreadrecipes.com

and join us on Facebook at:
www.facebook.com/RecipesForYourKitchenAppliances

www.ingramcontent.com/pod-product-compliance
Lightning Source LLC
LaVergne TN
LVHW020018041125
824975LV00009B/329